Confidence and Ignorance: 100 Things a Man Needs to Know

J.V. Bloom et al.

Published by J.E. Bloom and Sons, 2022.

CONFIDENCE AND IGNORANCE: 100 THINGS A MAN NEEDS TO KNOW

First edition. March 14, 2022.

Copyright © 2022 J.V. Bloom et al..

ISBN: 979-8201578022

Written by J.V. Bloom et al..

This book is dedicated to all the people that taught us life lessons, either through helpful words, or a smack across the butt. Although some were appreciated more than others, they coalesced to make us the men we are today. It is also dedicated to you, the reader, and your own journey. Special thanks to my daughter Sarah that proofread it with a unique vision.

Preface

We're fathers, brothers and sons from the south, and we thought that there was a need to pass our information along.

"To whom?" you might ask.

We made a list of things we thought were important for men coming up in the world. It came out of listening to eulogies and wondering what someone would say at our funeral, and concepts we thought might be important in having a good life. We stayed inside during COVID and argued with each other about religion, politics and the state of the world. That shaped what we thought was important, and helped us define our audience. This is written for men of any age that are ready to look for a little more. Whether you are looking for career advancement, self-actualization, saving money or simply figuring things out; we wrote this for you. We wanted to help educate you so that you won't make mistakes of ignorance and limit yourself. You can look up a lot of things online, but you have to know what you need to look for first.

It may not be for every culture, socio-economic class or age group. We tried to put things together that will help you if you agree. You may not be ready to get rid of your ugly wallet, or you might not value some of these tips. The good news is that it will be waiting for you when you are.

Before we dive in, I wanted to break everything down into two big categories. Confidence and ignorance.

You need confidence. That is what attracts people and makes you someone people want to know, work with and promote.

Ignorance is not knowing some important thing, like needing to wear a suit to a funeral. When people see you make a mistake of ignorance, they assume that there are many other things you don't know. It isn't fair, but it is life.

We hope that you learn how to exude confidence and remove ignorance through some of the simple concepts we bring up here.

1. Tip Big

Servers, bellhops, valet drivers, the guy that takes you from the long-term parking to the terminal, give them a few bucks just because you should. There are cultures where people don't tip and I get it. However, in the US, you have to tip because that is how the server gets paid. Using a coupon? Tip on the regular amount. Did the waiter comp your meal because there was a finger in your rigatoni? Tip them more. They will be working somewhere else soon. If you aren't a tipper, or you are a little unsure about when and how, listen. This is the exam for many of the notes we've given you in this book. It goes back to the having a good wallet, being aware of your environment and carrying cash. Don't be afraid to ask questions or do a little research online if you aren't sure of the amount. Keep ones and fives for drivers and bellhops, and tip your hotel maid more. If you tip a server in cash, it's more likely that they are going to get it, where a credit card tip might go through the owner first. Do it, it will make you a better person, and that is what this is all about

2. Keep Your Mouth Shut Most Of The Time

Numbers 2 and 19 in this book are a pair. *Keep your mouth shut* is the twin sister to *always be courteous to others.* The less you say, the smarter you seem. That is a fact that goes back to time eternal. If you don't say anything, it also makes people uneasy and they make mistakes – for my evidentiary submission I present Clint Eastwood in those Good, Bad and The Ugly movies. He was a bad ass and just stared at people. The more you can do that, and speak less, you'll have less to regret. If I had kept my mouth shut more often, I'd have been punched less, women would have cried less and I would have less things that kept me up at night. Learn from me.

3. Old Money

There is a joke about old and new money. Old money doesn't show off, old money requires that society follows outdated rules, old money has a beautiful home and impeccable taste. New money keeps her mouth shut when she wants to say F You. Rules like, "Don't wear white after Labor Day" come from people separating those who are in the know from those that aren't. Don't be like that. Be inclusive. Children that come from old railroad money are too afraid to spend it. They don't want to be the ones to exhaust the family fortune. A self-made millionaire is much more generous because he feels like he could make it again. I think that you should treat everyone with respect, whether they have money or not. In my personal experience, the ones with old money are no fun to be around. Mostly, I feel sad for them.

4. Be Fun To Be Around

Ever met someone that brought the whole room down with whatever came out of their mouth? Did you ever want to be around them again? That is the kind of thing you learn as you spend time around people in your formative years. If you don't know about it, let me spill the beans. When you are in a group of three or more, people typically don't want to hear about problems. They want to have a good time. Everyone has their own story, and in order for you to be asked back to the next lake party, make sure that you are pleasant to be around the first time you go. If you have problems with your wife, work or your brother, try to have those conversations with trusted friends, family or counselors in a one-on-one environment. Reading the room, emotional intelligence and not dumping your woes on others are key to getting invited back to the next party. That and bring booze or a delicious seven-layer dip.

5. We Came From Cavemen

If cavemen could survive 20,000 years ago, so can you. Learn how to start a fire, tie good knots and how to sneak up on things. We have some ancient ancestors that would be pretty impressed with our technology, but not our open fire cooking skills. If you weren't an Eagle Scout, read books and go do things outside to familiarize yourself with the world you live in and how to survive if you get stranded somewhere.

6. Don't Helicopter Parent

If you have kids, or plan to have kids, don't spend their young lives hovering over them. It is easy to worry about all the real and imagined dangers out in the world, but for the most part, kids will turn out ok, and a bump, scrape, or broken leg won't end them. Try and get them to go outside and do all the things they need to do to learn. They will make more mistakes and learn faster if you let them live their own life. I spent a lot of time outside because we didn't have video games or the internet. We live in a different world, but I can't see how putting on goggles and living in a virtual world is preferable to playing in the woods. Kids need some pushing to get off the couch and learn about the virtues about being the member of a team or how music will enrich their life. They don't all have to be chess masters or ballerinas. Be cool with your kids and they will be better for it.

7. Establish Your Dress Style

We can all agree that quality fabrics cost more, and that cheap shoes are instantly recognizable. This is more about how to say who you are through your clothes. I propose that you can wear different things, bathing suits through tuxedos, but you still have your own style that carries across. Like most things in this list, it is about confidence and taste. Can you pull off a pink blazer paired with white slacks and no socks, or are you more comfortable in a nice pair of jeans, crisp white button down and Tony Llama boots? All that is up to you, but consider the image you want to project. Are you flashy and want to be remembered at a social gathering for what you wore, or do you want to be understated and move seamlessly through the crowd? Think about that as you shop and build a wardrobe that you can be proud to wear. You can change pieces as you need to, but if you have a style, it isn't a chore.

Think about your projected profession or business as you pick your style. Compare the difference for the gynecologist or plastic surgeon with the car salesman. Pick a style that adds to your perceived value.

8. Get Stupid Drunk Before You Go Out Into The World

There is a school of thought that says you should get drunk at home; with people you trust so that you don't make a fool of yourself when you go out into the world. Basically, don't be thirty-five and not know how to handle your liquor. I made the mistake of drinking too much white wine in London and had a heck of time going to a work presentation the next day. I had a boss that got too drunk on a work trip and broke his eye socket. I am a big fan of never drinking enough to get a hangover or look like an idiot on a work trip or at a wedding. It comes with experience. If you are over 25 and you drink to excess frequently and it causes you to struggle in life, put this book down and go to an AA meeting. Quitting drinking is a great thing to do. If you go to a bar an order club soda and lime, no one will question it, and if they do, then they are the idiot and you can say anything you like to them.

9. Ask For Help

When I talk to people about my success, I frame it in one image: I've made every mistake and in the big picture, I don't know a whole lot. That is a great place to start. If you are fearless in your question asking, and asking people for help, you'll go far.

I've lost my job a few times, mostly because there was a poor plan at the top for making money. I needed help to find a new job. Job searching is its own book, but you need people to connect you to people that don't quite realize that they need to hire you. People who are hiring don't want to talk to candidates, but people that aren't hiring will almost always help you out. We all need each other from time to time, and connections while job searching is something people understand. When you are humble and genuinely ask for help, people help you. The ones that don't are the ones you want to avoid.

10. Don't Double Dip

At parties, there is an art to dipping, never double. In a large event, don't feel the need to thank the host. Get the hell out of there and send a note later. Be polite and introduce yourself to people, but try and read the room. I've been to events where I'm the outsider, and there is a balance to striking up conversation with people that aren't interested in what you have to say, and meeting new people. If it's not your crowd, be cool and hit the road. If they are welcoming and fun, invite them over to your place next time. Invitations lead to more invitations. Making friends is harder than it was in elementary school and you need all the friends you can get, brother.

11. Don't Wear Shoes With Holes In Them

Adlai Stevenson got an unexpected, but unsuccessful bump in his campaign for showing that he had holes in his shoes while running for president against Dwight D. Eisenhower. While he may have wished to be seen as 'the common man' when in reality he was a rich Illinois politician, that is not the same for you. Shoes require attention and one needs to keep them clean and in good repair. Good dress shoes continue to look good even with honest wear. Keep them looking clean and polished and you will be happy with the results.

12. Be Inquisitive

Continue to learn your whole life. Try and see the forest, not just the trees. When you disagree with someone, investigate why. You may not change your mind, or theirs, but at least you can understand. Just because someone has a public forum, doesn't mean they are correct. Read books, listen to people, and most of all, learn from your mistakes. People struggle with information today. Specifically, where they get their information from and what is correct. It's not enough to just point out what a dumbass they are, you need to get inquisitive and ask them questions about why they believe so strongly in something. I'm no therapist, but I imagine that the answer lies somewhere deep inside, like a need to hold on to power, or believe a narrative that they are put upon for a reason. You aren't going to change their minds or fix their problems. When they push back on you for believing something different, you aren't going to change your mind either, I bet. If you can't find common ground and keep from coming to blows, use my trick. Either say, "You might be right," or "I'm going to pray on that." One of those will work every time. You don't know most things, really, so don't be afraid to ask questions. You can be the expert next time

13. If You Can Remember Everyone's Name You Ever Met, You Could Be President

My uncle told me this one time, and I never forgot it. The thing is that people like it when you remember them. They like you for remembering them. I have one of those faces that people forget. I also remember everything, so this rings true for me. It's not fun to remind someone of when and where you met them, and if someone does remember me, I inherently like them better. Pay attention and remember people that you've had conversations with. If you meet someone out and about and you remember them, but not their name, try this tip. Stick out your hand and introduce yourself with your first and last name. "John Smith, damned glad to see you again." Hopefully they will shake your hand and say their name in return. That's what they are supposed to do. If they don't, say, "I'm sorry I've forgotten your name." Who knows, this might be a good pickup line. Your results may vary.

14. "Beer Fear" Is A Real Thing

The next day you will feel like the world has ended and you caused it. Just hide under the covers until 5pm and don't apologize. Everyone who drinks too much feels like that. If those around you hold it against you, then they are not your real friends.

Remember this feeling and how you want to avoid it. I have a rule that I can't drink more than two drinks in an evening. I always feel good the next day. If you want to go nuts, don't blame me tomorrow.

15. Learn To Accept Authority To A Degree

Biblical teachings propose this and state we must respect those in charge of us. If the system is too severe, leave and search for a better one. Internally we disagree a little on this one and it is generational. When things are going your way, and the system is just, it is pretty easy to accept authority. However, when you feel totally screwed over by "the establishment" then it is easy to imagine a radical change. Personally, I think that radical change is something that hasn't been embraced by biblical teaching in centuries, so maybe that isn't the guideline we need today. Here is what I think it boils down to: Don't do the crime if you aren't willing to do the time. This is whether you possess illegal drugs, drive drunk, kill your cousin in a shootout in your trailer or break windows out of the Capitol. You know what you should do and what you should not, so make good decisions. Nothing will derail your life like jail time

16. Plan Ahead For Special Occasions

Have gifts in the closet ready to go when you forget someone's birthday or special holiday. Send flowers for funerals, and bring gifts to weddings. Send little kids birthday cards with money in it. Give more than you get back and people will appreciate you for it. One tip I have is know how to say a prayer publicly. I learned years ago, and now I'm the go-to Thanksgiving, Easter and family dinner prayer leader. It's one of the few times I get to perform and I'm thanked for something I learned. That's valuable to me.

17. Tell Stories

Life is a collection of stories and it is a delicate balance to know how to cut them down to the right length. A good story is good to have at hand, especially in interviews. If you don't remember stories, sit down and write out your life story or start paying closer attention from here on out. Funny stories are always preferable to sad ones, but they each can play a part in the public speaking arena.

18. Children

Have them when you are ready to take care of them. People say that you are never ready, but let me tell you that you can absolutely have them too young, and they never save a failing marriage. Don't get a woman pregnant if you aren't planning to stick around and be a fantastic example to your child. You aren't ready for that? You aren't ready to take risks. Take the responsibility of preventing an unwanted pregnancy, don't leave it up to anyone else. I saw a note somewhere the other day, "If you can't pay the vet, you can't afford the pet." This applies to kids, but doesn't rhyme as well. You'll find out that when you have kids, you need to take care of them a lot more than you need to buy non-essentials.

19. Always Be Courteous To Others

Treat women with respect even if you're not sure they deserve it. Most of the time, she's going to be right and you will be the idiot. If you smile often and take verbal insults with a grin, people will wonder what you have up your sleeve. Maybe it is the knowledge that you are valuable regardless of what ever comes out of their mouth. A little bit of a detour here... a buddy of mine told me about this term: the halftime Flush. It is like the cardinal rule of riding a tour bus, *never number two on the tour bus*. If you have to drop a load at a friend's house, whether it is at a party or just watching a game, always mercy flush. You don't want to ruin the bathroom, so be cool.

20. Regrets

When I was a young man, I wondered what would have happened if I had taken different paths in life. What if she said yes instead of no? Now I know that is the stupidest concept in the world. What if? What a joke? That's some newspaper salesman line from 1873 when he ran out of papers to sell.

Here's the thing...you made a decision. Be a man and stick by it. Life is full of different doors and missed dates. If we can learn one thing from golf...the second shot is never significantly better scoring than the first. It's because it's a sequence of decisions. And your tastes improved. When I was a kid you wouldn't catch me dead eating a tomato sandwich. Now, I consider it delicious.

If you had different information, then you might have made a different decision. That fact is you didn't. So, stop lamenting in anguish.

21. Plan Early For Your Retirement Healthcare

The best story I've heard is a guy was an extra in SAG for 30 years and had healthcare for free. If you start early then you can get that part of life taken care of...which all people worry about in America. Or gain dual citizenship and pay taxes in the EU and get it for free. Don't forget to consider long term care after illness or injury. It is difficult to learn the best buy in such insurance. But give it some concern. Medicare does not do that. Maybe the VA is for you. Maybe you have reserves. I thought that Luis Rukeyser was informative about that need for retirement, but now he is gone.

You need healthcare to take care of your family, and you need a family to give you a purpose. Get to work on both.

22. Hair Style

Most men will probably lose hair as they get older. There is a secret. The more you lose, the shorter it should go. Everyone laughs at a comb over, even if he is the president. Don't get plugs or scalp reduction surgery, inevitably you'll end up with a scarred, bald head. Give in and put your vanity aside. Shorter is better as you age. Want to grow your hair to your shoulders? Do it before you turn gray.

There are also rules about having a beard. The three of us can grow great beards but would never think of having that long, lumberjack looking style that passes your shirt collar. It looks fun, but it is a pain in the ass to keep it looking good and like having really long hair, it just looks weird when you are doing normal things like running. People wonder what is chasing you. Classic and drama free, that's what we go for, but this is about you. Grow a crazy beard, or dreadlocks if you want, but remember this page if you find yourself in a situation where you regret it.

23. Climb Mountains And Swim Oceans

There is something to be said about independence and exploring the natural world in a contemplative, dare I say Mindful, way. This isn't a suggestion that you solo scale Everest to prove something, but that there are things you can do while quietly enjoying yourself outside of a club, cruise ship or group of friends. I still remember when as a teenager in New Mexico, I took the challenge of riding a brahma bull. It was a short experience but a lifetime of remembering. There is nothing quieter than swimming, snorkeling or scuba diving. You realize your own fragility and place in the world when you are underwater. It is similar for climbing. Whether climbing a rock face, or trekking a path to the top of a crest, you are away from typical distractions and you are offered a chance to examine the world around you. Go for walks, take a swim. If you don't know how to swim, put this down right now and learn. There is nothing worse than drowning needlessly.

24. Think Before You Insult

My Uncle used to say "Kill 'em with kindness". He had a colleague that was rude to him publicly. Instead of returning the insult or doing anything overtly sinister, my uncle sent the man a dozen roses. When the flowers were delivered to his house, his wife asked why he got a dozen roses. after he explained to his wife what he'd done, he grumpily realized the error of his ways and apologized.

25. When You Are Drunk

Get to safety, treat it like it's an emergency, because it is. You can ruin everything you've worked for with belligerent behavior. The best thing is to not be drunk; the second best is to not let anyone know. This goes for a ball game or a work retreat. We can't stress enough how important it is to stay in control. If you have too many, don't do anything stupid and be cool.

26. Tolerance

There are two slightly different definitions of the word tolerance. One is the ability to withstand something like a drug, or extreme environmental conditions without adverse effects. The other is to have the willingness to tolerate something that you don't agree with.

Being a man is about tolerance in both of these definitions. Need to take out the trash when it is cold and wet outside? It's your job, man. Every single time. Never ever make your wife do something that is unpleasant physical labor. It is your job. She puts up with you already, the least you can do is always do the dirty work, and do it with a happy heart. Show people that you do that kind of work without complaint, because you know where your coat is, or you are just tougher than everyone else, and you'll get that respect. And you will respect yourself.

Tolerate other people's opinions too. It has been a tough few years with half the country believing something that the other side doesn't believe. But be BIG enough to let them have their opinions just as you have. Just decide yourself what you believe. I have a lot of opinions on why this is, but it doesn't matter, because I'm not going to convince someone to switch political parties or take a vaccine.

27. Take Chances

Buy something that will grow in value. Start a side business or take a risk investing in someone else. We only get one life, so you might as well take it to the limit. Try and understand the difference between an investment and a rip off, but probably you'll figure that out with trial and error.

We have very different opinions about investing outside of your traditional 401k. One of us has big plans and tries big schemes. The other never takes risks. I dream of a just and verdant world where all acts of charity and kindness are rewarded and people that cheat or grift never win. Make sure that you are prepared to lose every dollar that you loan or give someone. That is going to happen. If you spend your life regretting your decision, you will end up being an old salty dishrag. I know some really rich guys that invested millions in an idea that collapsed in the Covid pandemic. They walked away quickly and easily because they were rich and understood the risks. That's the secret, understand what losing money means to you and your new, updated wallet.

28. Decide Your Go To Drink

Don't depend on the bartender to tell you what to order because there is nothing they hate more than stopping down to run through the list of all possible drinks just to have you choose a margarita, again. Figure it out on your own time. There are a million books and websites devoted to cocktails and you can determine what your go to drink is. I'll give you a hint: it isn't frozen, it is never blue or green, and if it is red, it is because it has grenadine or Campari in it, nothing else. Like fashion, simpler is always better. I'm talking about Gin and Tonic, Jack and Coke, Scotch or Bourbon neat, or on the rocks. A martini, a Greyhound or maybe a mint julep if you want to be crazy. Margarita is always a winner in the right setting. At the beach or on a private island, go for a Daiquiri. In my favorite city, New Orleans, get a Sazerac or a Hurricane.

29. Experience Physical Challenges

Try to participate in all opportunities even if you have limited abilities. You will find one to which you excel and that will also give you a broader knowledge as life goes on. Quoting a little Socrates (he was an ancient Greek philosopher, look him up), "...it is a disgrace to grow old through sheer carelessness before seeing what manner of man you may become by developing your bodily strength and beauty to their highest limit." This means that you should do all you can do before you get too old and creaky to run a marathon, bench press 250 pounds or chase down a purse snatcher.

Do enough to protect your woman and yourself, but no need to worry about being a hulk. Remember your legs and abs will lift more weight than your arms ever could. The real secret is to take caution over your joints and cartilage. All those body builders will be in wheelchairs at nursing homes with limp dicks. So, don't be a candidate for a penis implant surgery.

30. Have A Good Wallet

When your wallet gets worn out, replace it. This is one item that you should splurge on. Good quality materials that last a long time and never embarrass you are key when choosing a wallet. Like shoes, when they wear out, get a new one. Also, make sure to keep cash on hand. In a time where we are moving to electronic payments, having a few twenties in your wallet shows that you understand how the world works. They are good for paying people back, paying your share, greasing a palm or a generous tip that isn't shared by an unscrupulous owner or credit card company. If you paid for everything in cash, you'd have more of it. Also, don't store your whole life in your wallet, just the things you need.

31. Dogs Should Be Trained

If you have a dog, it needs to understand basic commands and not try to eat people or other dogs. A pet is a reflection of your home life. Are you scared, crazy, aggressive? That will all be crystal clear once we meet your dog. If you go somewhere and have your dog off-leash, every resulting problem is 100% your fault, no matter how good you think you have him trained. If your dog comes after me or mine in public, I will bite back, so be prepared.

32. The Key To A Good Golf Swing Is Try To Hit Through The Ball

Like life, just go easy and don't try to knock the cover off of the ball. People get mad as hell when they suck at golf. Yeah, what do you expect? It's golf. Golf and baseball are sports that track your errors. We don't track how many punches a boxer misses, we wait for the one shot that will knock the opponent's ass out! Treat things in life that track your errors like the stock market. It's just another trade. Get better with time, and take what you, and other people, have learned and incorporate that into your planning. I think that experience is the best teacher, but I hope to God you never have to experience killing someone to know that it is bad.

33. Diversify

Money is just green pieces of paper; however, you need them to buy delicious things. One of the things you should learn about is how to save and grow your money. There are strategies around investments in the stock market, real estate, businesses or annuities. We aren't investment planners and suggest that you get some real information and balance that against where you see the world going. Is the stock market too high, are homes overpriced, maybe you should hold in a cash position until that changes? Learn about dollar cost averaging and use it to your advantage.

34. Be Kind To Animals

If you hunt or fish, be respectful. Don't kill for sport, kill something if you intend on eating it, or if they are an invasive species. I know hunters that spend more time watching than killing. That is impressive. If you have a pet, remember that you are its whole world, and it depends on you for structure, food and love. Give it plenty. If an animal is suffering, help it. Get your dogs and cats fixed, and adopt if you can. If you can't afford the vet, you can't afford the pet. We are nicer to our dogs than we are people, and I can see why. We don't deserve the love that dogs are capable of. Cats, not so much.

35. Drinking Has Rules

When ordering a drink, stick to this rule: Brown liquor is for tough old men, Vodka is for skinny preppy dudes watching their weight, Tequila is when you are ready for jail, beer is for when you have to go back to work. Red, pink, green, blue or other colors, take a pass and insert a funny insult here. Don't mix any of these together. When at a business dinner, order one drink only if the boss does. Don't say I don't drink. Just order one. You don't have to drink it. On the other side of it, don't drink more than three. Your coworkers would love for you to slip up so they have leverage to keep you from being their boss. Fellas, when you order wine, order Red.

36. Fighting

Hopefully, by now you've had someone punch you for something stupid you did. It is one of the greatest teaching tools ever. You don't forget the first time you got your lip busted for being a smart ass. I think it is a great way to gain empathy for others. You don't usually get hit out of the blue. If you do, be very careful before you hit back. I see more women throwing punches in fast food restaurants these days. Still doesn't mean you can hit them back, but know how to block, disengage and if worse comes to worse, don't let one of them whip your ass.

37. Give Time And Consideration To Your Religious Beliefs

Establish your beliefs early and pursue them all your life. When you have a family, lead them in your religion and consider your role in church activities. Joshua 24:15: "But if serving the LORD seems undesirable to you, then choose for yourselves this day whom you will serve, whether the Gods your ancestors served beyond the Euphrates, or the Gods of the Amorites, in whose land you are living. But as for me and my household, we will serve the LORD".

Maybe you don't want to believe in anything, but we think that believing in a higher power has benefits. Religion brings you comfort, and shouldn't be used against anyone. You should do this for yourself, because you won't change anyone else's mind.

38. Using Nicknames

Nicknames are great when they are your friends, but know when to use them. A childhood nickname probably didn't stick around long enough to greet someone at a class reunion. In the real world, I have a commonplace first name, and a last name that lends itself to seemingly great nicknames. However, if someone I meet for the first time calls me a shortened version of my last name, I'm checking to see if he's drunk. If I want you to call me something other than my name, I'll tell you.

39. Ask Questions When You Don't Know Something

The goal of these topics is to prevent you from embarrassment. Some of the work you need to do yourself. One of the things you need to continue to do is to ask questions when someone uses a word, phrase or acronym that you are unfamiliar with. It is valuable in the workplace but also in everyday life. What if you didn't understand something and used it incorrectly in conversation? You'd look dumb, and you don't want that.

Here is a tip: Google is a great way to find things out and I met a young man that had a great way of searching. He'd literally ask his full question into the search field, compared to me typing in relevant disjointed terms, because I'd been using computers for way too long. The first time I heard him speak a complete sentence and get accurate results back I was stunned. Now I do it all the time.

40. Don't Stare At Women

This is about treating them with respect. Yes, we all know that every woman is beautiful and mysterious. You can look at them if they are in trouble, or if you are speaking to them, or if they are performing. If you look at them and don't want to be caught looking by them or the woman you are with, ask yourself something. "Should I be staring like this?" Sometimes you just can't take your eyes off of them. However, they already feel like they are being hounded. Don't be another pig that ogles a strange female. If you want to talk to them, do it. Be pleasant and respectful. If they don't want you around, respect it. No questions asked. If you are afraid to talk to them, avert your eyes. Give a stronger, more confident guy a chance because you need more time to work out and learn to strike up conversations. See how that fancy watch isn't helping at all?

41. The Most Important Thing In Life Is Art

You might think that it's food or money. Nope. Those are necessities, like drinkable water. What I'm talking about here is that once you've gathered enough to survive, you have time to focus on the good things in life. I've met many people that focus on science, engineering and software development in my career. The thing that keeps them sane is having one foot in the arts. Music, dance, visual arts, it doesn't matter, you need art in your life. Learn to appreciate it and understand the difference between what someone tells you is good and what you think is good. Sample different things so that you are well rounded. If the only music you know about is classic rock, or rap, not only will you seem dim at a party, you will be missing out on things that may bring you joy, and that is what life is all about. Learn, go to museums and concerts and spend time around people that know about and value art. It will make your life richer.

42. Apologize Sincerely

We are wrong more than we like to admit. Being gracious and giving a genuine apology to people that you've wronged or told you not to do something is a talent. Practice it. What I personally hate is when a celebrity or politician says something horrible in public, and you just know that they absolutely meant it, or their actions that they thought were completely right hurt people. When these media darlings give an apology that you just know is fake and only done at the advice of their business manager or lawyer, it is really shitty. Don't be like that. If you do something wrong, own it. Apologize because you know that you screwed up and then take that on as a life lesson. Maybe they will never forgive you but that's out of your control. What you can do is to be sorry and do better next time.

43. Turn Off News Channels

Wean yourself off of the 24-hour news stations. You will be happier by putting aside the opinion based, entertainment-driven, audience grabbing sensationalism. There isn't enough news to warrant 24 hours of it, so you end up with talking heads trying to divide and make you mad. People divide themselves politically based on whether they think it is truth or propaganda, and unfortunately the people that proclaim the loudest are usually the most wrong. You need to know about the weather, local events, scientific discoveries, and what is happening in the world. Learn to discern, listen to opposing views and know that you aren't going to change anyone's mind. If someone suggests that you storm the Capitol building or go to war in a foreign land, odds are they aren't thinking about what is best for you. Look for people with real answers, not complaints. Also, leaders that say you should follow and believe in them above all others are trying to start a cult. Watch out.

44. Bathe Often

I have worked with a few men that I had to pull aside and tell them that they smelled bad. One didn't apply deodorant and coworkers couldn't take it after noon, and the other had an issue with poor dentistry. Again, if people realize that you don't understand simple, polite hygiene, then they will think that there are other, bigger, things that you don't understand. Monitor yourself. Be clean. Wash and brush. If you are offered a breath freshener, take it as a hint for better oral hygiene. Have a nice haircut. Wash your clothes. Don't make someone else have to tell you that, because if they do, you can be sure that several other people put them up to it. It is a tough thing to tell a grown man, and only the bravest were chosen. Women that you aren't related to never tell you.

45. The Seven Deadly Sins

Pride, envy, wrath, lust, avarice, gluttony, sloth is the list, and they all exist in each of us. The key is to understand them and why they aren't good for you. You can look them up and read many texts on them. I like to think about them as something my grandmother would be against. Don't be lazy or eat too much. Treat your neighbor like you want to be treated and be a helper, not a jackass. She would have said that being envious, or angry that someone is doing better than you is the ugliest thing you can do.

46. Work Hard At Being Healthy

If you can't walk or fit in an airplane seat, fix it. It is easy to fall into a pattern of bad behaviors, or have an untreated medical condition that impacts your health, and it hurts to realize that you're not healthy. Make life changes as soon as you can. Being ten pounds lighter reduces the load on your knees by forty pounds. Get fit, you'll be happier.

47. Journal Every Day

One day you'll forget things, or when you die, people won't have a record of your stories. That's how we live on after we die: our stories. Start capturing what you do, where you go and who you see. Sorting out your thoughts on paper makes you a calmer, smarter, better and more literate. You can't accidentally delete a journal, so it will probably last longer than that presentation you worked on last weekend. It doesn't have to be a deep, psychological review of your grocery purchases, or an in-depth critique of what someone was wearing at Starbucks, but hey, it's a start.

48. Pass It Down

I've had to deal with a few estates recently and the one thing I've learned is that you need to pass wealth down to your offspring. Have a will, and make sure you leave things to your loved ones. When someone gets nothing from your estate, that's what they remember. Nieces and Nephews deserve a little something here and there. If you are fortunate to leave your children and grandchildren something, you should. Even better if you can do things when you are alive, just don't forget them. They need the things you take for granted. But most of all, remind them how much you love them. Leave them a note or a token of that love.

49. Be Aware Of Your Environment

You likely are not a Navy Seal or a Marine Pathfinder. But nevertheless, you must be aware that something may go amiss in your life. Traffic, weather, strangers, potholes, or yellowjackets may intervene to ruin your day or that of your friends and family. Stay aware of what is happening around you and you may save yourself time and injury. This goes for things as innocuous as standing in line, and letting someone pass by politely or watching or that car that is absolutely going to pull out in front of you. Pay attention and it will pay off.

50. Pay Your Own Way

Don't let people pay your way, or if they do, at least try to pay your own way. Never just sit there when the check comes. Pull out your wallet and offer up cash. If someone insists, say thank you. If you are broke, or too young to have your own money, I think that you would have a special arrangement before you go out to dinner. If I invite you and know that you don't have two nickels to rub together, I'll pay. That's why I invited you. But if you are broke and I don't know it and we agree to go someplace that you can't afford if we split the check...that's on you. Decline the invitation so that we aren't both embarrassed.

I had an old aunt that always put money in our hands because she didn't have any kids of her own. I thought that it was best to say, "No thank you," and decline the money. She gave me a stern lecture about accepting gifts graciously. You know what, she was right. If someone wants to give you a free meal, or buy you a beer, it is their gift to you. Say thank you and try to gift them the next one. Be generous and gracious, you'll go further.

51. Be Responsible And Have A Plan

Be a Man! If you are the head of the household, you have some responsibilities that are unspoken: Think about how to survive if there is no power, no water, no food, there is a pandemic that wipes out your resources. These need to be part of your overall household plan. In business we call it disaster recovery planning. Your household should have this plan, and you should have the skills and confidence to make it happen. People depend on you.

52. Take A Gun License Course

Guns are loud and shooting at targets is a way to get instant feedback on your skill. Whether or not you plan to own a gun, or want to carry it in public, take a course to learn how to handle one properly. They should have locks, and never be available to children. Be sensible about what you purchase if you do buy a gun. There is a lot of information out there about firearms whether you want one because you are afraid that someone might break in to your house, or if you are a deer hunter. It will teach safety and establish familiarity with weapons. Learn about how far a bullet will travel, especially through walls of your home. We have differing views on gun ownership and what is the best protection, and when one needs protection by firearm. I think a small gauge shotgun provides security and keeps you from accidentally shooting family members sleeping two rooms away.

53. Respect

Treat people that are serving you with respect. Whether a waiter, nurse or security guard, they are worthy, and if you don't treat them well, not only will others notice it, you will be a jerk. If you are a jackass to these people, others will notice and respect you a lot less than those you are demeaning. Everyone has way more value than you realize, and no one is actually enjoying serving you. They are working to make a living, chase a dream, or pay off a debt. You aren't important enough to complain about anything. If you want to point out a problem to the management, do it after you leave.

Never forget that people don't actually care about you as a customer. They are in it for the money to buy food and care for their families. You are just a customer, and probably wrong most of the time.

54. If You Want To Be Great At Something, Practice

It is hard to practice, and at first you think that it is a waste of time...suck it up and keep at it. One secret is that you don't have to give it 100% all the time, sometimes showing up and going through the motions is enough to learn something, but consistency is the key. Great doesn't always mean that you win. There is always a better guitar player, golfer, or ball player out there. The key is to be great for yourself, and get just a little applause from those around you.

55. Don't Hesitate To Have Tough Conversations

The longer you wait, the harder they get. Unfortunately, I'm an expert in having the tough discussions, even though I don't like it most of the time. (I'm a shit-stirrer, so sometimes I do like it. Go figure.) Coworkers actually appreciate it when you tell them that they stink and need to take a shower. When someone is getting laid off, and you have to tell them, it doesn't get easier by waiting. You need to think how you'd like to hear it and go do that. They are either going to hate you or not, you can't control that, but you can control what you say, how you react and that you are recognizing that this discussion sucks. Sucks for them, it doesn't matter how much it sucks for you, because you aren't getting laid off...just yet.

56. Learn How To Dress Well

When you buy clothes, there are two categories, Branded and cool, or a little more expensive and classic. Pants rarely change, so if you are on a limited budget, pick a classic style and spend money on the shirt or accessories as fashion changes.

If you can find a smaller, high quality men's store, and find the owner, you'll have someone that you can trust to dress you well. It will cost more, but you'll look good. You can get out of a Macy's with some good things, but they won't pop like some of the smaller labels do.

I don't care what you wear, but I want you to know the difference between good and cheap, Classic and out of style by next year. You wear different things on stage than you do in the boardroom, so think about where you want to go, and plan ahead.

57. Travel

Go places and see things. Leave your state and your country to learn how other nations and peoples live. Those who never leave will miss many adventures and the chance to learn about life. There is more out there than you know and you owe it to yourself to see things and talk to strangers. When you are in a foreign land, eat their food and do as many local things as you can. Staying on a cruise ship keeps you from the real experiences.

Traveling is the best way to learn tolerance. I'm not talking about getting off a cruise ship, ruining the local ecosystem and economy and making people hate you. I mean go places and see things and talk to locals. There is no better way to understand a culture than to visit. Today, we have so many armchair pontificators that hate a given group of people, but haven't left their own borders, or even their own state, and they become xenophobes due to blissful ignorance. When your neighbor complains about immigrants, foreigners or other nations, ask him if he has travelled there and give him the same advice. The best meal I ever had was in southern Germany with people that spoke no English. I'll treasure that meal for a lifetime.

58. Never Buy Anything That Is A "Luxury Brand"

Good quality beats a label every day. There is a difference between a luxury brand like Gucci or Louis Vuitton and a well-made brand like Allen Edmonds. The luxury brands don't hesitate to make products that wear out. In either case, you want to spend your money on something that lasts, makes you proud to wear it and isn't overpriced for the logo stamp that was added in a factory. Handmade is great and I recommend buying from artisans and craftsmen whenever possible because supporting them is a wonderful way to give back to the economy. Supporting products made in a factory with low wage earners is not. The only thing I would splurge on would be a standard Rolex, or if my wife wanted a fancy purse, I'd get her one. Thankfully, she does not.

59. Act As Though Your Actions Will Appear On The Front Page Of The Newspaper

This is something I learned when I worked at Disney. It wasn't about me, it was about saving the corporation money. Now we are talking about you as a person. Don't embarrass yourself by doing or saying something that you wouldn't want written on the front page of the newspaper or your favorite digital media news app. Hopefully these pointers we are giving you help you grow so that you don't do something stupid because you don't know better, but really it is up to you.

60. Language

What you say, how your accent works and your knowledge of language is the key to moving forward in life. When writing, understand the difference between there, their and they're. If you use an idiom, make sure you know what the hell it is. Nothing is dumber than messing up a phrase because you don't know it. I'm reminded of Nate on *Ted Lasso* who said, "Wonder Kid" instead of "Wunderkind." This points out how important reading is, and asking questions fearlessly. I always ask questions about acronyms at the office because I secretly hate them and how people toss them around to be classist. Also, not every other word needs to be the F-bomb. If you have to curse, at least be eloquent about it, there are some great phrases out there that go unused.

61. Learn To Drive A Stick Shift

There are seemingly fewer and fewer manual transmissions available for sale. There is a joke that says a stick shift is a great theft deterrent. You need to learn how to drive one because one day you'll have to...and you may need to show your daughter how it is done, along with changing a tire.

62. Watch TV With Captions

There is nothing like a good bank building exploding during an action movie to wake your sleeping baby. Getting used to captions not only helps you keep the volume low when you need to be quiet, it helps kids to learn to read quickly. I learned that Finland had the highest literacy rate because they didn't have dubbed cartoon voices. Everything was subtitled, and in those generations, kids were the best readers at an early age. Even though I don't have little kids, I hate watching TV without captions. With them, I get everything the characters say.

63. Know At Least One Good Joke

I have a buddy of mine that is the most outgoing, fun-to-be-around guy you will ever meet. He is famous for good jokes and laughing at himself. I know a few jokes, but the ones I never forget are the ones I can't tell in polite company. Do better than that and learn ones that aren't embarrassing.

64. Friends

Having friends makes you healthier. Not only because you can go and do things with them, but they are people that you can socialize with too. Don't neglect your mental health. A good party can make you happier than just staying home and watching TV.

The key to going to parties is to have parties. You invite people to things; they will invite you to things.

I have a friend that is the greatest friend that ever existed. He keeps in touch with everyone. Phone calls, cards, gifts and he has a network of people to travel the world with and stay with. There is nothing like visiting friends, so make a ton of them.

I knew a professor at Johns Hopkins and he had many students over the years. He sent each one of them Christmas cards each year and kept their addresses. Of course, these graduates became Professors and Chief of Service at many institutions. He subsequently developed many influential friends of long standing to share many stories. He said that one year there was to be an eclipse of the sun that could be seen from the beach in Maryland. He sent a message to these friends that he would be in a beach chair with a helium balloon lofted from his chair-no other message. As the sun arose a large crowd surrounded him to observe the phenomenon.

People can have different levels of friends: those they know well and would put as their emergency contact, and then people they see from time to time and are friendly with. I know people that consider and treat everyone as a great friend. I tend have a smaller number of good friends, but I am always open to making a new one. Sometimes we don't know what is going on in someone's life, and they may not want to be a friend or not know how. Try not to take this personally, and be friendly to everyone you meet. It will pay off in the long run.

65. Learn How To Tie A Bow Tie

Styles change and often one does not use all the talents he acquires. In regards to dress however, it is beneficial to learn certain skills and appear to understand them. The long tie can be tied in many different knots-Windsor, four in hand, half-Windsor, Shelby, and others. These are not difficult to tie and do not wait for your girlfriend to do it for you unless that is a special desire. Have this skill and practice it in private from time to time. Be confident. Also, it is a special skill to know how to tie a bow tie. This is just like tying your shoelace but on your neck in front of a mirror. Google can show you how and if you learn, you will be ahead of your competition and the 'hero' of many style gurus.

66. Keep Jewelry To A Minimum

This isn't to say that you can't wear any jewelry, but you need to monitor how much you wear. If you are an entertainer, and choose to wear multiple chains on stage, that's your choice. However, for most people, jewelry is a way to make a subtle statement to people that are looking. Make sure that you give the statement that you want in the accessories that you wear. Personally, I have a watch and a wedding ring. That's it. When I see a man with a bracelet, I try to figure out why he is wearing it. Was it a gift or memento from a trip to a tropical island? Did he think that silver bracelet made him look tough? Does he need to wear a lot of rings because he is going to be on stage right after this job interview? I rarely ask, but the stories are there.

67. Anxiety

It is an ancient feeling, related to our cave-dwelling ancestors being stalked by a predator, and yeah, we all have it. We are telling you all of these tips to cut down on some of your anxiety, but no one is going to be prepared for everything. The secret to shaking off your anxiety is to get into action. So, get to work. Do you need to make a scary phone call, or have a conversation with a human when you are a lot more comfortable texting? Make that call without a second thought. By the time the phone is ringing, you aren't anxious anymore. Every single time I have recollected on a time where I was scared or anxious to do something, I realized it was 100% me worrying and not anything about the issue. Turn around and face that tiger, tiger.

68. Send Flowers

Write thank you notes and send flowers to every funeral. It might seem like a pain until you have a loved one die and read the cards on the arrangements. People do care, and you should be one of them. Don't talk yourself out of it, just step up. Send gifts to weddings, and buy birthday presents for loved ones. Whenever you get a gift, write a thank you note, they are classy and impressive and let the giver know you received and appreciate it. There are three things you need in every thank you note: the observation, the impact and then appreciation. Look it up if you need help. Finally, always let the giver know that you received a gift. I have a relative that I have to track down and see if the package arrived. That's not cool.

69. Politics Don't Matter

It is easy to get riled up over left versus right. This is because the American two-party system is classist and designed to divide the people so that the ones in power stay in power. You can do your part by not fighting but talking. Always vote, but do your research. I was a fool and voted for a Senator that I didn't realize was 85 years old. There is a reason they want to stay in power when they should be long retired. Let's work together and make things better.

70. Complaining Doesn't Get You Far

Part of life is sucking it up. You are going to lose from time to time. Understanding the long-term goal is the best way to avoid the anguish behind short term failures. Hitting rock bottom is probably the best way to understand the struggle and what is important. Turns out Money and Fame are not the best goals in life. Friends, family and free time beat them every time.

When you run into issues in life, there is a difference between a complaint and working to solve a problem. If you came to me with a complaint, my first human reaction would be to tell you to suck it up. However, if you had a suggestion to fix whatever caused your complaint in the first place, well now I'm listening.

71. Military Service

One of us says, "If I could, I would spend 2-3 years in the military to serve my country. Would you?" The other served his country in Vietnam and doesn't talk about it much. The third never, ever wants to have to kill another human being on behalf of a politician. You probably have already signed up or not, since our average readership is past draft age. However, I do know a guy that joined the Air Force in his 50's. Go figure. A military education can be a great fulfillment to a man. He learns discipline, orderliness, and self-deprivation. But when that is not desired, it can be painful. One can learn to work with other men, and women now, which is beneficial and often skills are learned that transfer to the civilian occupations. Don't discount joining the Military but take care, and if engaged, go all out.

72. Don't Wear Pajamas On A Commercial Flight

There was a time when people flew in style. Hats, suits, gloves, it was a fancy event. Today you see people dressed like slobs and fighting in the aisles. You don't have to wear a suit, but don't wear workout clothes either. Look smart wherever you go and you will be better off for it. You'll meet nicer people when you look good. I like wearing layers with lots of pockets when I fly.

Back in other times, my wife and I were mysteriously picked from the loading line and conducted to the front where we were told we had been selected for a First-Class seat! We were also told we were picked because we were dressed like we belonged there. Who knows?

73. Eyeglasses

Unless they are readers or just for fun, never get cheap glasses. They show. Unfortunately, glasses are a monopoly, cost too much and it is hard to select the right frames for your face. However, if you take the time to shop, get professional advice on face and frame shapes, you will get a lot of compliments. A woman stopped me on Bourbon Street to tell me how much she liked my glasses, that's the goal, fellas.

74. Don't Be A Picky Eater

Nothing brings a dinner party to a screeching halt like a picky eater. If I knew you were a picky eater, I'd never hire you because it shows you are fearful or had bad parenting. Why don't you like vegetables, or sauces? Maybe you need to talk to a therapist about it. If you are Kosher, or vegetarian, that's your choice, and I don't consider that picky. There are things that we all don't like to eat. For me, it's organ meats. The point is that you don't want to make your host work too hard to accommodate you. If you are vegan, don't demand it at a party of non-vegans. Eat before you come, and find things you can eat. Try new things all the time, especially if you are in a new location. Go to local places to eat and try the regional cuisine at your host's table. You will be better off for it. If you are picky, and can't get over whatever your parents did to you, hide it from everyone. I mean it. Don't bring food to someone's house. Eat in advance or just lie and say you have horrific irritable bowel syndrome or something. Anything is better than being fearful of eating what is put in front of you. Once you are over 12, you can't order chicken nuggets or mac'n'cheese in public. And above all, don't criticize what someone else is eating. That is not your prerogative.

75. Make Plans For The Future

When you are 20, make lofty goals and reach for the stars. Get it out of your system. Within your 20-year plan, expect that you will need to change your career. The days of one career or job are over. In your 30s be working towards a diverse skill set so you're not caught flat footed in case of a layoff and in financial jeopardy. Retirement will most likely require some career change so you don't lose your purpose. I like the idea of multiple sources of income so that you aren't chained to a desk for your whole life.

76. Learn Self Defense

If you ever have to use it, don't inflict pain, but know that you can protect yourself. That is the kind of confidence that people are drawn to. I am confident that I can take a punch, but I also know that people can kick my ass. That correlates with the advice above. Keep your smart mouth shut so that you don't get your ass kicked. If offered the opportunity to take a boxing lesson as a young man, don't turn it down. Learn a few wrestling holds and escapes and try Judo.

77. Become Proficient In Something

Pick at least one thing to learn and practice so you can become proficient in something-music, history, golf, tennis, pickleball; it doesn't matter what it is. Learning a skill gives you confidence when you encounter new things. If you have a practiced athletic ability, other sports will come easier because you are fit and fast. Know how to play the piano? Other instruments will come easier. If you are great at tennis, the hand/eye coordination translates to other things well. The more you learn to do, the more you know about doing new things and you are able to have fun learning them. That is what life is about.

78. Dress Simply

We talked about style and not buying labels just to have a label, but this is my personal opinion. Don't be a peacock, unless that's your jam! When I see a man in a mustard-colored suit with matching shoes, tie and shirt, I wonder why. Was it a bargain, or is he going on stage? Guys over 20 that dress like skateboarders or old men with sleeveless T-shirts are missing a chance to show that they have the capability to be intelligent and worthy of respect. If you dress like you don't know some key information, people will assume that there are a lot of other things that you don't know. It isn't fair, it is just how the world works. Clean, well-fitting clothes that are occasion appropriate are very important. Again, you don't have to drop a lot of money for a fancy logo. In fact, you should avoid logos whenever you can, unless you are being paid to wear them. Dress simply and impress people. It is kind of like keeping your mouth shut when you don't know the answer. You seem smarter.

79. Polish Your Shoes

I can't stress good shoes enough. There was a guy I worked with that was a software engineer. He seemed to have one pair of black shoes, and he wore them like slippers, with the backs crushed down. They must have cost $14.99 originally and they looked old. These were his go-to shoes that he wore every day. I noticed, and so did everyone else. He got no promotions, no accolades and was let go quietly in a round of layoffs, because people questioned his abilities to do more than the minimum requirements. He didn't get it, and I hope that you do. You don't have to dress in the finest things, but you need to have nice things. Know how to polish your shoes, and when to polish them. Style fits into shoe polishing. Some shoes need a bright shine using the Marine Spit-Polish technique. Others require the old Cream use. Learn the difference and use one as appropriate. People notice.

80. Don't Pee In Public

Just because you can, doesn't mean you should. Don't ever pee on a wall in a public place. What are you, an animal? Jesus, I saw a sign that said to not pee on the side of a building. We shouldn't need signs to tell us that. Plan ahead. One of my most fragrant memories is coming into New York City through Port Authority. Public restrooms are underrated. Clean up after yourself when you finish in one. No one wants to clean up after you. No one.

81. Money

Don't ever discuss how much you make with others. Until we get to a point when everyone's salaries are public, discussing yours will only lead to unhappiness for you or the person listening. The only exception is if you and your co-workers discuss salaries in order to determine if your employer is paying fairly. If you are rich, try not to let it be known. Be generous with what you have, not ostentatious. If you want something fancy for yourself, get it only if you will feel comfortable wearing or driving it anywhere. Remember that Mr. Walton of Wal-Mart fame, drove his used truck and dressed plainly most of his life.

82. Be A Mentor

Don't offer free advice, it's only worth what you pay. Instead, provide perspectives that challenge the younger generation. Be confident that whatever is blocking this younger person will pass. That is what they need from you- reassurance. They get plenty of gloom and doom from their electronic devices. When they get to a crossroad that concerns them, let them know that either decision will most likely yield a similar result though it seems hard to understand from their current perspective. Life is like a mulligan, the second shot lands in a different place, but doesn't make much difference to your total score. Just like where we land later in life.

83. Get Comfortable With Mechanics

It's key to know that most Mechanics only replace parts. So, don't fear speaking with them. You are a customer, and if you don't find a mechanic that will listen to your concerns, shop around. Do a little research on cars and ask questions when you take it in for repairs. Working on your own car will help you to understand the value of a good mechanic and deciding if you want to do it yourself.

84. Confidence

This should be top of the list. Confidence is the one thing you need to get you through life. Believe in yourself and others will believe in you. It's not about lying; it is the opposite. Be confident in yourself even when you don't know the answer. Be confident in your decisions, especially when you deviate from the norm. How do you get confidence? Good decisions, and lessons are learned from bad ones. I have done so many things wrong, that there isn't much left to screw up. I can spot a con, a dangerous situation and an opportunity because I've lived through them. Learn things and trust your gut and you'll do just fine. Keep your mouth shut more than open and you'll seem smarter. Learn to Listen!

85. Buy A Home

It doesn't matter whether it is a cabin or a loft, it will provide you with tax relief and a place to invest your money. Like a car, you can work on it and not kill yourself. If you don't have a lot of money, get one out of town or somewhere cheap. It will rival your retirement savings and may beat it as long as you don't buy at the top of the market. Do your research before you make any big purchases. Losing your home is a huge hit to your credit rating.

If I had to do it all over again, I would take my first five grand and immediately buy a half-acre of land. Sit on it. Pay taxes. Cut down the trees. Level it and over the years park my awesome trucks and atv's on it. When I saved enough, build a pre-fab home on it. Why? Because you can rent it. You can write off taxes against it. You can sell it 20 years later and possibly make money on it. You can mine it for gold. You can drink beer on it. Growing up, I always thought buying property was expensive. But it's only expensive in retail environments. Get as much land over time as you can. Build a little place that you are proud of on it and sell it...to buy more land. Stocks go up and down, land does too, but at least you can walk it.

86. Tattoos and Piercings

I try to avoid them. To me, tattoos are permanent and you are in a bind if you get something you regret, or in the worst instance, misspell. I see young men with complete sleeves that look interesting, but I am sure that they have times that they make sure they keep their long sleeve shirts down, because it just doesn't seem right for every occasion. I see brides with lots of tattoos, and I wonder what they will think about as they show their grandkids. For me, I don't have a need to show off any art. If I ever got a tattoo, I fantasize that it would be a pirate ship in a stormy battle at sea, across my entire back. That way I could wear a shirt and no one would ever know. Piercings seem like outward manifestations of a need to be just a little bit different, while actually being quite common. Like pinky rings and bad bracelets, it is better to keep jewelry to a minimum.

87. Take A Motorcycle Training Course

Face it, riding a motorcycle is fun, but it isn't a matter of whether you crash, but when. A course is cheap and short and will build confidence for the next time you ride, or when your buddy offers to let you ride his bike. The courses available today convert a novice to an intermediate in three days. This adds confidence which can be used for many events-even aiding automobile driving.

88. Keep It Inside

Farts, burps or rumors. Those are things you'll wish you did in private. I believe that many, many people regret things they said to people or about people. If you were trusted with someone's secret, keep it. If you did something wonderful for someone, keep it anonymous. What is the purpose of saying how much you donated to charity or a guy begging on a street corner? You are a better person inside for keeping it to yourself, that is what that whole Bible verse is about. Those that crow loudly usually suck.

Taunting or insulting strangers is also a bad idea. Getting into a fight at a ball game might seem fun until you have to deal with the ramifications of it. Be the bigger man and let things go. Try hard to appreciate the other person's situation before taking up an issue. Everyone has some concern that cause them to enter into a fuss. Smile more than show your fangs.

89. Read Literature

Read all the time. You will learn things about life and you will be able to have better conversations at dinner parties. Fiction is a must, and history will help you understand where you came from and why life is the way it is. If you don't develop deep roots in your culture, you'll never get to the heart of things. I say take self-help books with a grain of salt. But read the classics. You will find that they are honored because they are good in many respects and often teach life-lessons.

90. Speeches

You'll have to give them. Learn 3 and practice them before other people volunteer and don't look back. You will regret not being prepared when it is time to talk in public. It doesn't have to be good, but it has to be done. Please don't read it off a piece of paper. We hate that.

I'm going to put public prayer (dinner table or holiday meals) in this group. Here is the secret to making them good.

Start with a memorized template. It is up to you to find one, but there are things out there that are good examples of a wedding toast, or something you'd say at a wake. Steal that, and write it down. Next, make holes in it, like where you'd add someone's name, or the event or the reason you're gathered together. Then make space to say whatever is relevant and funny. That you remember the dead guy because of the time he gave you a wedgie in seventh grade, or how you thought your sister would never find anyone to marry. Then go to the closer, this is the most important part. It must be uplifting and memorized. Keep it short, tight and funny.

91. Strive To Be Non-Judgmental

Realize that others have a history of their own and were led to their position in life. Keep in mind the mantra, "they all put their pants on one leg at a time". One thing I keep in mind is that "Everyone is in their own movie." Think about it. People have their own stories, problems and things that they are dealing with. We can't know someone else's mind and we put all our interactions with others through our own lens. If you think about it like we are actors in their movie, just playing in this scene, then you realize the scope of your interaction with that person. Are you in their life and a supporting cast member, or are you just placing your order with them, and just a few seconds of their movie? We can't know what others are going through, so let's give them the benefit of the doubt and let things play out. My barber used to tell me to Let it Go. It took a while to understand what he meant. I think he means that all the fake stuff that people do like buy Teslas or fancy watches is bullshit. Do what you like and let the rest blow in the wind. "Love thy neighbor" is often a difficult command, but one worthy of recall.

92. Make The World Better

A goal for all of us is to make the world a better place when we leave. Even though divorced billionaires are going into space at a fervor we've not seen before, this blue ball is all we have. Treat it with respect. Don't litter, don't create oil spills or toxic waste. Recycle and plant trees. If you get into public office, try and stop bad things from happening instead of taking money from corporations that don't have our best interests. I try and pick up after myself, buy things that will last, and catch and release. You might do something different but do something. It's not anyone else's responsibility.

93. Buy Less

I've said it before, but we live in a consumerist society, and companies are doing everything they can to get you to buy something, anything. Be aware that large and small merchandizers are most excellent at identifying what you will purchase and convincing you to do so. They use AI for marketing and make it "too easy" to use credit. Be on the defensive and do not let your family shame you into submission. Take a long look at what you really need: another streaming service subscription, a new car, a three-hundred-dollar hoodie? You can do whatever you want, I'm not your mom, but I will tell you that you will find things that bring you real joy, so put some aside to buy those items and experiences. Get things that bring you joy, not things that you think will make other people envy you. They don't care. People are more impressed with how fit you are, or pleasant, or freshly groomed. No one cares about your watch.

94. Own A Suit

Many of today's men do not own a suit. The needs for one may be few in your job and entertainment. But you should have one that fits well and is conservative in tone and color. You may actually wish to own several suits in addition to the sport coats and slacks you select. In the past, books were written on "Dress for Success" and "Clothes Make the Man". You will be surprised how many doors you open by dressing neat and in 'your style'. Whether it be women, employment, or asking for a loan, your appearance offers you advantage in many ways. You need to have a suit that fits and is in style for two main reasons: weddings and funerals. You plan for weddings, you don't for funerals. It takes a few days to get a suit altered, that's why you need to have one in the closet, so you look sharp at a funeral. It is called paying respects for a reason.

I had a neighbor who was a successful individual who knew how to promote himself. He was quoted as saying, "Don't go into a bank for a loan looking like you needed one."

95. Say Hello

Introduce yourself by name to everyone you meet. An etiquette hallmark that has faded is people knowing how to introduce each other. If you go to a party and no one introduces you, do it yourself and remember that person's name. If you are introducing someone to a close friend, remember to introduce the most important or senior person to the lower ranking person, if that is appropriate. Add a little something that they might have in common or that would be a conversation starter. This makes you a good host or friend and people will want to be around you. Another tip: If you've met someone before, but can't remember their name, stick out your hand and tell them your name, they might just tell you their name back. If they don't pick up the hint, be honest that you forgot their name. That gets it out of the way quickly.

96. Explore Education Early In Life

Do you need college or would technological skills satisfy your career goals? Not everyone needs to go to college for a fulfilling career, but you do need education to understand things, discern things that are important and understand all the things that you don't know. Pursue the total education as early as possible rather than trying to 'catch up' after you have full family responsibilities. Some of the smartest people I know don't have a long formal education. Maybe they were the smartest because they got right to what was important to them. You will find reward in seeking education in some form all of your life.

97. Automobiles Are Not Investments

A car is a liability. Unless you are a fortune teller and bought a sought-after '71 Plymouth Superbird and kept it in a temperature-controlled garage for 40 years, they will not go up in value more than a modest mutual fund. The minute you drive it off the lot, you are underwater and you should buy it because you love it, have enough money, or you need it-and you have enough money. Personally, I don't want to buy a Tesla for 90k, when I could get something serviceable for 15.

Their job is to get you from point A to point B, but we give them more value than they have. They are rarely an investment, and as soon as you buy a new one, you are losing money. A wise man once said, "If you want to drive, you got to pay." I had a car that was luxurious, but every time something happened to it, it cost way too much for parts.

Get something that you feel good driving and can afford to keep up, but know that no one else cares if you have the latest truck.

My cousin's ex-husband bought a new Ford pickup and then instantly decided that the newer Dodge was better, so he traded it in. Soon they were divorced and broke.

98. Learn Basic Facts About Wines Even If You Do Not Drink

You will go to a restaurant and someone will ask you about wine. You need to understand red vs white, dessert wines, and regions that wines come from. California is a good start for wines, Georgia and Texas are not. I personally like a full-bodied red wine, more Merlot than Cabernet, and don't care for white wine or champagne. My father is a fan of discussing a nice Riesling from Germany, but sometimes you can't go wrong by knowing what you don't know. I can't memorize every vineyard and type of grape, but I can ask my server or sommelier for a recommendation because I already know that I like a boring, full bodied red wine. I like a beer better, but I know when to get fancy. Learn a little and be confident enough to ask for help.

99. Listen Closely When People Are Selling

Whether it is cars, houses or the house special, sales professionals typically tell you the type of people they are in the comments between their pitches. Then you can know if you can trust them or not. I recall the pleasant men selling life insurance to medical students and how they were the nicest people on the block. They wined and dined students and told them how they would be wealthy and successful in a few short years. Yet, when the policy was purchased, or not, that pleasantness vanished and they became distant and perhaps just another inebriated soul.

100. Be Prepared To Pay

This is the topic that inspired me to start this project. When you are paying for something, don't rely on Apple Pay or whatever you have on your phone to work. Be prepared with credit cards or cash. If I have to stand and wait while you transfer money back to your debit card, I might just kick your ass. If you don't want to carry cards or cash, stay home.

When you go out to eat and the check comes to the table, pull out money. I don't care whether someone else is going to pay for it, be prepared to pay. That is what men do. I have experience of paying for tables of people, and I know who appreciates it and who takes it for granted. I also know when I owe you and you owe me. You don't want to be on the wrong side when the time comes.

Finally, if you borrow someone's car or truck, return it full of gas. Period. Anything less and you are a jackass.

Epilogue

You become a man once you pass about thirteen years old. You won't feel like one then, that is just what some people say. The government classifies you as a man when you turn eighteen, but you are still pretty dumb. You can buy beer at twenty-one, but I maintain that you aren't much smarter than you were when you were eighteen. You might have more experience at things, that's all. Getting married or having kids are the kind of milestones that turn you into a man and help you realize it is about people depending on you, and your ability to be present and be dependable. There are a lot of things you need to know to be a good man, and even more to be a smart man. Keep learning everything you can. Read a lot, and spend time with different people that are smarter than you are. Ask questions and look things up. Keep your mouth shut most of the time, and when you do speak, don't say mean things.

We wish you the best, and look forward to the man you become.